MW00897291

The Aroma of Worship

Written by Derin A. Stidd

Edited by Connie Dennis

Cover Design by Dwight DePalmer

Disclaimer:

The statements in this book are not intended to diagnose, treat, or cure any disease. For medical advice please seek out the council of a licensed medical professional.

<u>Acknowledgements</u>

First, and most importantly I want to give thanks to God, who for the purpose of His own glory, purchased my salvation through the blood of Christ on the cross, and now is constantly at work in my life through the presence of His Spirit conforming me to the image of Christ. Let this book, more than anything else, bring glory and praise to Him.

I want to say thank you to Connie Dennis for her work editing this book. She is truly gifted with words and did an amazing job of taking my ramblings and turning them into interesting and coherent thoughts. Thank you to Dwight DePalmer for designing the book cover and for encouraging me in this endeavor. Thank you to Lori Borre, who made the off-handed comment, "You should write a book," which was the catalyst for even considering this project.

I also want to thank all of the people who reviewed the book and provided feedback. James and Stacy McDonald, Ryan and Kim Prather, Brian and Amanda Friedl, Jacob and Sarah Adamo, Verick Burchfield, and Andy Jenkins, thank you all so much for your time commitment, encouragement, and thoughtful consideration. You are all truly contributors to the final product of this book!

To my pastor, James Farrar, thank you for helping me stay theological grounded, holding me accountable to stay the course, and reminding me to resist the urge to compromise.

Finally, I want to say thank you to my family. You all are the inspiration of the majority of what is written in this book. The stories and any wisdom present are because of all of you. If it were not for my children, my parents, and my brother and sister, I would probably not have anything useful in this book; and, it would certainly be less entertaining. I want to add a SPECIAL thank you to my wife who willingly and graciously sacrificed countless hours of my time in the production of this book. You are truly a helper whose worth is valued beyond silver or gold. You are my first editor, my idea assassin, and my most trusted counselor. Thank you for all that you have added both to my life and to this book. I love you!

What others are saying about the Aroma of Worship...

"The Aroma of Worship is not just another devotional, but rather a tender instructional on a different dimension of worship that has been lost to many of us. Reading this will help to unlock yet another amazing way to use your essential oils and will help you to have a more complete understanding of what it means to truly worship God."

Jacob Adamo, Author of Full Spectrum Success

"Aroma of Worship will have you really considering and worshiping God with all your senses! Derin helps us to understand that using our sense of smell is a great way fully worship God!"
Ryan & Kim Prather, Young Living Diamond Leaders

"You will love The Aroma of Worship as a devotional tool. By incorporating essential oils into the reading of scripture, Mr. Stidd shows the reader how to relax and get into a more worshipful mindset to experience their time in the Word of God."
Verick Burchfield, Young Living Crown Diamond Leader

"This book is biblical and thought provoking. God's word coupled with aromas that facilitate an attitude of worship. This will make an excellent Christmas gift for friends and family!"
Brian Friedl, Young Living Platinum Leader

Table of Contents

Foreward

I love it when people find an area they're passionate about, link it to their essential oil business, and let things simply flow... as a natural expression of who they are. There's a passion and grace and simplicity in it all in one. Ideas flow naturally. And it's contagious.

I remember the first time Derin and I talked about his idea for this book, about how he wanted to introduce - or reintroduce - people to several of the essential oils (and particularly some you've seen mentioned in the Bible, but might not have even known were essential oils!). He mentioned he wanted to tie the ideas to Scripture, make a few "real world" comments, and invite people into a multi-sensory experience with their Father.

He wanted them to know Him - in their heads. That is, He wanted them to have the information.

He also wanted them to feel Him in their Spirit - to become aware of the great love Paul described when He wrote that the Holy Spirit was poured into our hearts (Romans 5:5).

He also wanted them to sense Him - to actually, tangibly "feel" the physical oils and to smell the very things He had created to bless His children.

As Derin spoke more and more about his idea, I was drawn in. That's what happens when people talk about something they clearly love!

I thought, "Yes! People need this. The love of the Father isn't just something to know in your head or experience in your spirit, but it's also something to feel... to physically encounter."

Think about it.

We are five-sense beings. We see. We hear. We taste. We touch. We smell. The Lord gave us each of these senses for our good and His glory.

So, read Derin's book and open your senses as he discusses the smells, the aroma of worship.

Feel the cuts on the Boswellia Carterii tree as frankincense - and healing – is poured forth from the very thing that would seemingly bring pain (isn't that life!).

Touch the hyssop. Remember, it was with the hyssop branch that Moses instructed the children of Israel to brush the blood of the lamb over their door posts (Exodus 12:22); it was with the hyssop branch too that Jesus was given a sour drink when he said, "I thirst" (John 19:29). As Derin writes, it's the hyssop that brings cleansing…

In the ancient world, essential oils were their medicines. It's what they had. In Jesus' day, then, healers would have walked around with a small bag attached to their waist-belt with small bottles of oil.

Did Jesus use essential oils?

Probably… yes. Think about it. The wise men brought Him three gifts. Two of the three, frankincense and myrrh, are well known for their healing properties.

Does this lessen the magnitude of His miracles? Far from it. Rather, it invites us to connect to His past in the present moment, seeing and touching and smelling the same experience those who physically met Jesus must have encountered.

So, as you weave your way through Derin's book…May the Lord bless you and keep you. May His face of great grace and favor shine upon you. May you go slow… and savor and enjoy the experience waiting for you.

Grace to you,

Andrew Edwin Jenkins
WeOverflow.com

Introduction

Why I wrote this Devotional

There are three primary reasons that I wrote this devotion. My first and most important reason is to share the Gospel of Christ with the essential oils community. As such, I have made every effort to point, in some way, to the Gospel of Christ in each devotion. Secondly, I want to communicate to the broader Christian community, through the medium of devotional writing, that the sense of smell, as well as all of the other senses, is a gift from God given to us that we may bring Glory to Him by using it to enjoy His creation. God has blessed us with this wonderful sense and He is worthy that we may intentionally use it in our worship of Him. Finally, I want to communicate in a very practical way that essential oils can be used in many ways that are consistent with the Christian worldview and to reject the notion that one must embrace New Age thought to benefit from essential oils. These are my goals; and, my prayer is the Spirit of God will see fit to use this work to that end.

What to Expect Each Day

Each day you will find: a brief instruction about preparing your surroundings and your heart, a passage of Scripture, and finally some additional thoughts about the Scripture for that day.

I have given some detail here in the introduction about preparation so that each day's instructions will be unique to that devotion.

Prepare Your Surroundings

To avoid distractions and promote focus, find a quiet room/area. Keep your Bible, this devotional, a journal, pen and highlighter near your chair. Also, set your diffuser up with distilled water. Each day's devotion will tell you which oils to add to your diffuser for that day. After adding your distilled water and oils to the diffuser for the devotion, start your diffuser and let it run for a few minutes before you get started.

Prepare Your Heart and Mind

Get comfortable and breathe in the aroma for a few moments. Clear your mind of cares that take your attention away from focusing on Christ. Breathe in and out slowly. Allow your senses to fully experience the aroma. Let the tension go out of your body and begin to focus your attention on Christ. Spend some time in prayer of adoration. Celebrate God in your own heart and worship Him. Thank Him for the specific aroma you are experiencing, for its benefits, and for your sense of smell which He has given you as an avenue of experiencing His blessings in creation. As you are wrapping up this time of prayer, transition into reading the Bible passage. Meditate on it. Read it out loud repeatedly and let the words resonate with you. Focus your mind on word, then concepts, and then complete thoughts. Allow your mind to take in what the text is saying. Read it until you have a good awareness of what it is saying both in your heart and in your mind; then, move on to the devotional.

God's Word

Each day you will find a Bible passage that will be the focus for that day. All Scripture references are taken from the English Standard Version.

Worth Thinking About

This section has my stories, thoughts, and devotional ideas relating to the Bible passage(s) and essential oil(s) for that day.

Holy Anointing Oil

(Myrrh, Cinnamon Bark, Cassia, Aromatic Cane)

Prepare Your Surroundings

Find a quiet room and set up your diffuser with distilled water. Add 4 drops of Myrrh, 2 drops of Cinnamon Bark, and 4 drops of Cassia. Aromatic cane is an oil called Calamus. Young Living does not sell Calamus. That's okay though, because we are not trying to produce the exact aroma; rather, we want to get the general idea. If you don't have Cinnamon Bark then simply add a couple drops of Frankincense in its place. Start your diffuser and let it run for a few minutes before you get started.

Prepare Your Heart and Mind

Get comfortable and breathe in the aroma for a few moments. Clear your mind of cares that take your attention away from Christ. Breathe in and out slowly. Allow your senses to fully experience the aroma. Let the tension go out of your body and begin to focus your attention on Christ. Spend some time in prayer of adoration. Celebrate God in your own heart and worship Him. Thank Him for His blessing of senses. Consider all of the ways that your senses are a blessing to you daily. As you are wrapping up this time of prayer, transition into reading the following passage. Meditate on it. Read it out loud repeatedly and let the words resonate with you until you have a keen awareness of what it is saying both in your heart, and in your mind; then, move on to the devotional.

God's Word

"The Lord said to Moses, 'Take the finest spices: of liquid myrrh 500 shekels, and of sweet-smelling cinnamon half as much, that is, 250, and 250 of aromatic cane, and 500 of cassia, according to the shekel of the sanctuary, and a hin of olive oil. And you shall make of these a sacred anointing oil blended as by the perfumer; it shall be a holy anointing oil. With it you shall anoint the tent of meeting and the ark of the testimony, and the table and all its utensils, and the lampstand and its utensils, and the altar of incense, and the altar of burnt offering with all its utensils and the basin and its stand. You shall consecrate them, that they may be most holy. Whatever touches

them will become holy. You shall anoint Aaron and his sons, and consecrate them, that they may serve me as priests. And you shall say to the people of Israel, 'This shall be my holy anointing oil throughout your generations. It shall not be poured on the body of an ordinary person, and you shall make no other like it in composition. It is holy, and it shall be holy to you. Whoever compounds any like it or whoever puts any of it on an outsider shall be cut off from his people.'" Exodus 30:22-33

Worth Thinking About

Have you ever taken time to consider how much our senses are a blessing to us? Consider them. There are five senses: taste, touch, smell, sight, and hearing. Each of them is a blessing to us in its own way; and, collectively they are a blessing to us because it is through them that we experience creation. Through them we are able to appreciate everything from a well-orchestrated symphony, to the scrumptious flavor of a gourmet meal, to the anticipation that comes from the aroma of brownies cooking in the oven. What a blessing these things that we call senses are to us!

Have you ever pondered why God gave us senses? Consider what the Bible says in Colossians 1:16, speaking of Jesus, it says, "For by Him all things were created, in heaven and on earth, visible and invisible, whether thrones or dominions or rulers or authorities - all things were created through Him and for Him."

Why did God give us senses? For the purpose of His own glory. More specifically God gave us senses so that through them we might worship Him. That reality is abundantly clear in our passage for today. In the book of Exodus God commands Moses to use a blend of essential oils to make what would be called "Holy Anointing Oil." This blend of oils was used to anoint almost every piece of furniture in the Tabernacle, and it was used to anoint priests. God was very specific that it was not to be used on any person, other than a priest; and, it was not to be used for common purposes. Every time the nation of Israel gathered to worship the aroma of Holy Anointing Oil filled the worship gathering.

God had a very specific purpose in doing this. He was teaching the nation of Israel that this aroma was the aroma or worship. This concept is a difficult one for us to grasp as westerners because we typically don't engage the sense of smell in our formal worship. But, the sense of smell has a very powerful effect on the brain. Of the five senses, the sense of smell is the only one that is processed through the emotional part of the brain before it goes through the logical part of the brain. This means that the sense of smell has the ability to create a certain response in our brain prior to our logical consideration. Often this response comes in the form of a memory, or a strong emotional response to a certain aroma. God made use of His beautiful design to engage the Nation of Israel in worship through the sense of smell. This Holy aroma, as much as sacrifices, laws, and rituals, was a part of their corporate worship. It was the part of their worship that engaged the sense of smell. Because the scent passed through the emotional seat of the brain, the activities of worship were reinforced!

The ability to experience the sense of smell is an amazing blessing from God. The fact that He can use our sense of smell to draw us nearer to Him is yet another example of His amazing grace poured out on us in His created order.

Take some time today to intentionally worship God through your sense of smell. Intentionally experience the aromas that you encounter throughout your day. God has given you a sense of smell that you may find joy in His creation; and, through that joy you might worship Him. Go and celebrate God's use of aroma to bring about joy in your life today!

Reflections…

The Gift Giver - An Important Warning

Prepare Your Surroundings

Find a quiet calm place. Set up your diffuser with Lemon essential oil and let the oil diffuse for a little while before you start your devotion time so that the aroma is in the air.

Prepare Your Heart and Mind

Start your personal worship time by just taking a few moments to breathe in the uplifting, refreshing aroma of Lemon. Spend some time in prayer thanking God for His creation and provision of such a pleasant aroma. Spend some time thinking through other ways that God has provided for your needs; thank God for them one by one and don't rush this process. The most important element of this devotion is spending time thanking God for His goodness. The actual devotion itself is of secondary importance to your prayer time.

After you've taken time to be thankful, read the following verse. Consider what it says word by word until you get the entire meaning in your head. Read it over several times. When you have a good sense that you understand what it is saying, then close your prayer time and move into the written devotion.

God's Word

"Whoever loves pleasure will be a poor man; he who loves wine and oil will not be rich." Proverbs 21:17

Worth Thinking About

When I was a kid one of my favorite times of year was my birthday. I mean, what kid doesn't love his birthday right? I remember sitting in the middle of the living room floor, bubbling over with anticipation and expectation as each new present was given. In my family we always followed the same pattern: the biggest presents were saved until last. The anticipation would build more and more with every package. For this reason, I had a tendency to rip through the first and smaller packages in a hurry to get to the next one. This caused my mom to establish the routine of constantly asking me, "What do you say?" before she would hand me the next present. Her expectation was that I would look around the room, find the person who gave me the present, and offer my most sincere, "Thank You!" My mom did this because she realized that as a child I had a propensity to be so excited about the gift that I would often forget to be grateful to the one who gave me the gift.

One of the interesting narratives that we see all through Scripture is when it comes to blessings from God, we have a propensity within us to celebrate the gift and forget about the gift giver. In fact, in some cases we can even worship the gift instead of the gift giver. The Bible calls this behavior idolatry. Idolatry is when we worship something other than God. Idolatry is a sin of worship and often perpetuates multiplication of sins. What we actually worship in our heart is the greatest predictor for our actions. For example, if we worship prosperity we will do anything we can to gain prosperity. If we worship power we will do anything we can to get power. But if we worship God, then our lives will be about bringing Him glory.

The reason I bring this principle up related to essential oils is because if we are not careful it is easy for these amazing gifts from God to take the place of God in our lives. We can get so excited about essential oils, and all the amazing benefits they bring to our lives, that we begin to invest all of our time, energy, and effort into things related to essential oils. It can be easy for people to go from celebrating God's goodness in providing essential oils, to cutting God out and just celebrating (idolizing) the oils!

The greatest tool in the battle against idolatry is a grateful heart. God is so good and we have so many blessings from Him to celebrate. This starts with the Gospel. God is so good that He sacrificed His Son on the cross to purchase our salvation. Essential oils are great! However, essential oils are a gift, and it is important for us to remember to be grateful to the gift giver.

Consider your own life. Have you allowed other things to creep in and get between you and God? Maybe you've gotten so excited about essential oils that you've forgotten they are simply a great gift from a great God. Spend some time today examining yourself. If you have allowed idolatry of any kind to creep in and take the place of God, then turn from your sin and ask God to forgive you. Remember all of the amazing blessings God has given you! Start with the Gospel and continue by considering all of the good things in your life. Remember the greatest tool in the battle against idolatry is a grateful heart. A grateful heart comes first and foremost by remembering what Christ did on the cross.

Reflections…

Frankincense

Prepare Your Surroundings

Put a few drops of Frankincense on your hands and rub them together. Now cup them over your nose and breathe in the Frankincense several times.

Prepare Your Heart and Mind

Allow your senses to take in the aroma. As you are doing this, try to put distractions out of your mind. Focus your mind on Christ. Let your mind connect the sweet smell of Frankincense with the time you are spending with The Lord. Focus on His crucifixion and resurrection. Think on the Gospel. Breathe slowly and deeply. Then go into a short time of prayer. Pray for whatever is on your heart. Read the verses below and pray through them. Meditate on them. Don't rush into the devotional. This part is more important. Just take a few moments to sit with the Lord.

God's Word

"I have said these things to you, that in me you may have peace. In the world you will have tribulation. But take heart; I have overcome the world." John 16:33

"And we know that for those who love God, all things work together for good, for those who are called according to his purpose." Romans 8:28

"Everyone then who hears these words of mine and does them will be like a wise man who built his house on the rock. And the rain fell, and the floods came, and the winds blew and beat on that house, but it did not fall, because it had been founded on the rock. And everyone who hears these words of mine and does not do them will be like a foolish man who built his house on the sand. And the rain fell, and the floods came, and the winds blew and beat against that house, and it fell, and great was the fall of it." Matthew 7:24-27

"When they had preached the gospel to that city and had made many disciples, they returned to Lystra and to Iconium and to Antioch, strengthening the souls of the disciples, encouraging them to

continue in the faith, and saying that through many tribulations we must enter the kingdom of God." Acts 14:21-22

Worth Thinking About

God is the grand designer of all creation. From the vastness of the universe that we see when we look through the telescope, to the intricate complexity we see when we look through the microscope, God is the creator and sustainer of it all. Because He is the author of creation, we often find truths about His nature and wisdom for daily living within the order of His handy work.

Hidden beneath the branches of Boswellia Carterii is one such truth. Boswellia Carterii is a small stubby looking tree that grows naturally in Somalia. The tree doesn't look like much on the outside. Its leaves are small, thin, and do not provide adequate coverage of its branches. As a result, the tree has a very shabby look, almost like a toddler emerging from their bedroom with a pair of scissors and a fresh new haircut. On the surface, the tree doesn't seem very valuable. It isn't beautiful. It doesn't provide any shade or shelter. Its leaves do not provide a good source of food or medicine. Additionally, it is a rather picky plant that doesn't grow well in most parts of the world.

Yet, beyond the shabby appearance of Boswellia Carterii, underneath the scant leaf covering and stubby branches, lies a treasure so valuable that it's greatness has been recognized as a symbol of prosperity, used as a source of trade, and even offered as sign of honor to great and mighty kings. This great treasure is a resin known as Frankincense. Almost since the dawn of recorded history, the sweet aroma of Frankincense has been celebrated as a gift from God to minister to any number of physical, emotional, and spiritual ailments of man. It has been used in the worship practices of countless religious observances, including those of the Jews and ancient Christians. It was offered to the Lord Jesus by the wise men from the East as a gift of worship at the time of His birth. Over the course of history, it has been one of the most valuable resources known to man.

But here's the catch, the only way to get this life-giving, affliction-healing, sweet-smelling resin from Boswellia Carterii, is to cut the tree. Specifically, to harvest Frankincense you must slash the bark of the tree and wait for the resin to seep out and harden. When the resin seeps out and hardens this is called a "tear;" and, it is only when the resin becomes a "tear" that it can be harvested and used. Are you beginning to see the spiritual reality that comes from this physical process yet?

Because we live in a world that is cursed by sin, and we are ourselves are sinners, there are things in this world that cut us. Things like death, disease, natural disasters, persecution, hate, and the list goes on. Jesus clearly and repeatedly taught that His followers would face these hardships. The parable of the houses teaches that each house, whether built on a solid foundation (Christ) or a weak foundation (anything other than Christ), faced the same storm.

The Author and Perfecter of our faith was nailed to a cross in obedience to the Father. He died in our place. Jesus took our sin upon Himself and faced all of the judgment that was intended for us. He then rose from the dead and now sits at the right hand of the Father.

Jesus calls upon us, because of His grace and mercy poured out on the cross, to follow Him in the same kind of radical obedience. In this world, we get cut up. We become wounded. These wounds, though they are painful for a season, are ultimately gifts from God. In the multitude of our tears, God brings forth the evidence of the marvelous changes that are happening under the surface. God, in His merciful love, changes us from the inside out as we read the Bible and pray. We can liken this to the priceless resin of God's grace pouring out of us through our worldly cuts. Our lives can then shine before others, in good times or bad, as a testimony of God's love.

Are you cut today? Go to the cross. Rest in Jesus. Let Him use your wound to bring about His grace and mercy in your life in ways that you never thought possible. You will find strength and solace in His refuge. Be a vessel of the resin of His grace. He loves you. You can trust Him. He will restore you.

Reflections…

Sacred Mountain

Prepare Your Surroundings

Put a few drops of Sacred Mountain in your diffuser and let it run. Also, put a drop of Sacred Mountain on your hands and rub them together. Now cup them over your nose and breathe it in several times.

Prepare Your Heart and Mind

Allow your senses to take in the aroma. As you are doing this, focus your mind on Christ and His holiness. Breathe slowly and deeply. Then go into a short time of prayer. Thank God for His perfect plan of redemption carried out by Jesus as the willing, spotless, worthy Lamb of sacrifice; and, praise Him for the wonderful gift of His Holy Spirit who is living and working in our hearts. What an amazing, sacred gift!

God's Word

"Woman, believe me, the hour is coming when neither on this mountain nor in Jerusalem will you worship the Father. You worship what you do not know; we worship what we know, for salvation is from the Jews. But the hour is coming, and is now here, when the true worshipers will worship the Father in spirit and truth, for the Father is seeking such people to worship him. God is spirit, and those who worship him must worship in spirit and truth." John 4:21-24

Worth Thinking About

When I was a kid I would get in trouble for running. I wasn't running to any place in particular, I just enjoyed running, jumping, and spinning in circles. I have never been good at sitting still. To this day, I still have a significant inclination to rock if I'm sitting still for too long. As you might imagine this constant desire to expel energy earned no small amount of trouble for me. One of the places that I frequently got in trouble for running was at church. Every single week I would be running through the church; and, every single week some sweet old lady at the church would stop me and rebuke me, "Derin Stidd! This is the house of The Lord! We do not behave that way in the house of The Lord. This is a special place and we do not run here!" Of course, I would reply with a quick, "Yes ma'am," walk just long enough to get out of sight, and then start running again! I would repeat this same pattern until someone finally grabbed my arm and dragged me kicking and screaming to my parents.

It's probably the repetition of this occurrence that was the greatest contributing factor to my enormous indignation when I later discovered that the church building was just that, only a building. My poor youth pastor didn't know what he was getting himself into when he taught this lesson. I believe the conversation went something like this:

> *Me*: *GASP* "You mean to tell me that the building itself isn't a holy place?!?!"
>
> *Youth Pastor*: "No it isn't. At least not according to Scripture."
>
> *Me*: "So you mean to tell me that I got in trouble for running in the church all those times for NOTHING!"
>
> *Youth Pastor*: "Yea I guess so... though I hadn't really considered that application point."

Jesus had a similar, though more serious encounter one day with a woman that he met in the course His ministry. This woman was a Samaritan and she was known for being sexually promiscuous. Jesus uses the analogy of water to draw her into a discussion about eternal life. When He asks her to go get her husband the woman tries to tell Jesus that she isn't married; but, Jesus isn't deceived. He tells her that He already knows she has had several husbands and the man she is currently living with isn't her husband. Upon hearing this the woman makes an interesting statement. She says *"Sir, I perceive that you are a prophet. Our fathers worshiped on this mountain, but you say that in Jerusalem is the place where people ought to worship."* (John 4:19-20) Now the woman can obviously see that Jesus is a Jew. She would also know that one of the greatest areas of disagreement between Jews and Samaritans was that of worship. In an attempt to divert the attention off of her sin, she presents Jesus with a controversial theological question. Jesus gives her a compelling answer that is the source of our discussion today. He says *"Woman, believe me, the hour is coming when neither on this mountain nor in Jerusalem will you worship the Father. You worship what you do not know; we worship what we know, for salvation is from the Jews. But the hour is coming, and is now here, when the true worshipers will worship the Father in spirit and truth, for the Father is seeking such people to worship him. God is spirit, and those who worship him must worship in spirit and truth."* (John 4:21-24) This is a ground breaking statement in Jesus day. First, He doesn't tell the woman that she can't worship because she is a Samaritan. Also, he tells her that the issue of worship is not going to be determined by location, but rather by the condition of one's heart.

This is consistent with the rest if Christ's teaching throughout His ministry. When Christ died on the cross the veil between the Holy of Holies and the rest of the temple was torn. This signified that God's presence was no longer going to dwell in a *location*, but rather in the *hearts of His people.* There is no such thing as places that are in and of themselves, "sacred;" but, as you go about living your day to day life, every place that you go is sacred if you are worshiping Him in spirit and in truth!

As you go about your daily routine today, remember the aroma of Sacred Mountain. Let it be a reminder to you that as a worshiper of the Most High, you ARE a "sacred mountain" carrying the presence of the Holy Spirit with you every place you go. Make it your goal today to be a "sacred mountain" to everyone by using each opportunity to display the glory of His grace at work in and through you.

Reflections…

The Oil of Gladness

Prepare Your Surroundings

Find a quiet place to pray. Open up essential oil bottles of Myrrh and Aloes (Sandalwood and Cassia). Start with Myrrh. Hold the Myrrh under your nose and take several deep breaths, then follow the same process with each bottle. Next put a drop of each oil in your hand, rub your hands together, cup them over your nose, then take several deep and shallow breaths. Enjoy the sweet smelling aroma! If you don't have these three oils, you may want to substitute the blend produced by Young Living called, "Joy™."

Prepare Your Heart and Mind

As you are breathing in the aroma consider the Bible verse for today. Take some time to consider what it means to have a glad heart. Consider the sweetness of the many relationships that God has brought into your life. Don't rush through this time. Focus your thoughts on the idea of having a heart that is glad in Christ. Once you feel like your mind is set on Christ, then move on to the devotional.

God's Word

"Oil and perfume make the heart glad, and the sweetness of a friend comes from his earnest counsel." Proverbs 27:9

Worth Thinking About

If you're like me, you may have had people say all sorts of crazy things to you when they discover that you use essential oils. I've gotten everything from, "Are you some kind of hippie now?" to, "Essential oils are used by the New Age Movement and are therefore the tool of the devil. You shouldn't be using or promoting them!" Much of the debate centers on New Age theology and spiritualism that is often associated with the use of essential oils. In some cases these objections may be legitimate and should be taken into consideration. Christians need to be cautious that they don't accidentally embrace New Age theology in conjunction with the use of essential oils. We should be careful that our understanding and our speech related to essential oils is Biblically informed and doctrinally grounded.

On the other hand, many of the objections raised against essential oils are not actually Biblical objections, but Western, Modernist objections. In other words, it's common for Christians to label something New Age that isn't actually New Age; it just isn't normal to them. Take, for instance, the premise that essential oils can have an effect on human emotions. As a pastor I have noticed that this claim is probably the most disputed claim among Christians. Usually the argument is stated something like this, "The claim that essential oils can bring about joy is a New Age claim and isn't consistent with Scripture. After all, the Bible teaches that joy is the fruit of the Spirit. Are you trying to say that essential oils can replace the Holy Spirit?" Of course we are not trying to say that essential oils replace the Holy Spirit. In this case, as well as all other cases, it is important for Christians to go back to the Bible as our ultimate source of authority. How does the claim that certain essential oils bring about happiness, gladness, or joy square with the teaching of Scripture? Consider the following passages:

Isaiah 61:1-3

"The Spirit of the Lord God is upon me, because the Lord has anointed me to bring good news to the poor; he has sent me to bind up the brokenhearted, to proclaim liberty to the captives, and the opening of the prison to those who are bound; to proclaim the year of the Lord's favor, and the day of vengeance of our God; to comfort all who mourn; to grant to those who mourn in Zion— to give them a beautiful headdress instead of ashes, the oil of gladness instead of mourning, the garment of praise instead of a faint spirit; that they may be called oaks of righteousness, the planting of the Lord, that he may be glorified."

Proverbs 27:9

"Oil and perfume make the heart glad, and the sweetness of a friend comes from his earnest counsel."

Psalm 45:7-8 ESV

"You have loved righteousness and hated wickedness. Therefore God, your God, has anointed you with the oil of gladness beyond your companions; your robes are all fragrant with myrrh and aloes and cassia. From ivory palaces stringed instruments make you glad"

You will notice that both the Isaiah and Psalm passages are prophetic passages that point to the coming of the Messiah. In each of these passages, the concept of an, "oil of gladness," is being used symbolically to communicate the healing ministry of Jesus (Isaiah 61:1-3) and the special favor that was on Jesus from God the Father (Psalm 45:7). The fact that these passages are speaking symbolically doesn't take anything away from the point about the oil of gladness. Symbolism is a literary device in which an author uses a literal reality to communicate a deeper, and often times, spiritual point. In other words, both of these passages teach that there can be a sense in which oils bring about emotional comfort, and even happiness. On the other hand, Proverbs 27:9 expressly and directly says that oil makes the heart glad.

Upon review of the Word of God, is the claim that certain oils promote joy an expressly New Age claim? No. In fact it is a claim that is very much consistent with Scripture. This conclusion may be troubling to some; but, that may well be because they have confused Biblically grounded truth with Modernist, Western assumptions. Of course it's also important to note that neither we, nor the Bible, are trying to make the claim that oils replace the Holy Spirit. The joy that is brought about by the Holy Spirit is an eternal joy that literally transforms a Christian's view of life. Oils don't do that. When we talk about oils promoting joy (or gladness), we are talking about joy in a temporal sense related to the way that the oil interacts with the brain. This is an important difference.

God is an amazing God, and in His providence and provision He has seen fit to provide for many of our needs, including emotional needs, in creation. Spend some time considering God's provision; and, take some time to thank Him for all He has provided for you!

Reflections…

Hyssop

Prepare Your Surroundings

Put a few drops of Hyssop on your hands and rub them together. Now cup them over your nose and slowly breathe in and out. Enjoy the sweet smell. Let the aroma fill your senses and take some time to begin focusing on Christ.

Prepare Your Heart and Mind

Once you feel as though your heart and mind are fully focused on Christ, transition into a time of self-examination. Ask God to show you where you are not experiencing total surrender to Him in your life. Consider sins of action and sins of inaction. Be honest with yourself and ask the Spirit of God to show you where you may be missing the mark. After spending some time in self-evaluation, begin to read the following passages. Read them, slowly and deliberately, out loud. Allow yourself to take in every word and contemplate the meaning. As you put the words together consider the meaning of the whole text. Do this until you have a good understanding in your heart and your mind of what the text is communicating. Do not rush through this portion. What God's Word has to say to you is far more important than what this devotion has to say to you. Take your time. Then transition into the devotion section.

God's Word

"Purge me with hyssop, and I shall be clean; wash me, and I shall be whiter than snow. Let me hear joy and gladness; let the bones that you have broken rejoice. Hide your face from my sins, and blot out all my iniquities. Create in me a clean heart, O God, and renew a right spirit within me. Cast me not away from your presence, and take not your Holy Spirit from me. Restore to me the joy of your Salvation, and uphold me with a willing spirit." Psalm 51:7-12

Worth Thinking About

The smell was unpleasant, strong, and all encompassing. I was in the Black Mountains on a youth leadership retreat preparing to go whitewater rafting. I first noticed the smell when we boarded the bus provided by the rafting camp to transport us to the water. It was a faint smell; but, it hung in the air almost as a prophetic message of things to come. At this point I didn't realize what I was smelling, just that the odor was present. As I stepped off of the bus at the rafting facility, my nose was greeted with an even stronger and more breathtaking version of this scent. Upon entering the facility the stench became more like the punch of a heavy weight boxer, constantly assaulting my nose with every hesitant breath.

Finally, I had to ask! I looked at our guide and exclaimed, with the little bit of breath that remained in my lungs, "WHAT IS THAT SMELL!?!?!?" She smiled at me and said, "That is the beautiful smell of whitewater!" From this point on everything reeked of this rancid odor of whitewater. The wet suits we put on reeked. The head protection we wore reeked. The boats that we carried and sat in reeked. But worse than all of these, when we finally were in the water, the whitewater REEEKKKEED! As we rafted, we fell into the water and it splashed all over us. By the time it was all said and done, WE reeked of whitewater. On the way home I remember having the thought, "I don't think I have ever felt so disgusting in my life." That thought played on repeat in my head for the entire two hour drive back to the camp.

Have you ever experienced this kind of uncleanness before? We find David swimming in this level of filth as he authored Psalm 51. Of course, his uncleanness is not of a physical nature, but rather of a spiritual nature. You see, this Psalm was written by David right after the Prophet, Nathan, confronted him about his adultery with Bathsheba, and his murder of her husband Uriah. In the midst of his pleading with God for spiritual cleansing and forgiveness, David makes this statement in verse 7, *"Purge me with hyssop and I shall be clean. Wash me and I shall be whiter than snow."* In this prayer for restoration we see David appealing to a physical reality (washing) to symbolize that he was in desperate need of spiritual cleansing. In Old Testament times, hyssop was commonly used on both people and objects for the purpose of cleansing. It actually seems likely, based on the words that David is using here, that he is appealing to the process outlined in Leviticus 14 for the restoration of a man who had been healed of leprosy. He was first to be cleansed with hyssop, and then he had to be washed, and then he was allowed to return to the camp. David is appealing to God to cleanse him in the same way that the leper was cleansed, so that he can be restored to God. Of course, we know from the rest of Scripture that God was merciful to David, and that God did cleanse and restore him.

Wrapped up in this psalm is the truth that hyssop is a symbol of cleansing. Within its aroma and its physical properties, we find a powerful reminder of God's gracious mercy toward us through Christ's death on the Cross. Jesus died that we might be cleansed of our sins. The Bible teaches that just like God was merciful toward David, He will also be merciful toward you and me. In 1 John 1:9, the Bible says, *"If we confess our sins, He is faithful and just to forgive us our sins and to cleanse us from all unrighteousness."* To confess your sins means to go to God saying the same thing about your sin that He says about your sin.

Take some time to think about your own sinfulness. Go to God and confess your sins. Thank Him for Christ's death on the cross on your behalf. Don't rush through this time. Thank God for His grace and mercy. He loves you! He wants to free you of your sins! Celebrate His goodness. Let God draw you into confession and listen to the guiding of His Spirit.

Reflections…

Lavender

Prepare Your Surroundings

Put a few drops of Lavender in your diffuser and let it run. Also, put a drop of Lavender on your hands and rub them together. Now cup them over your nose and breathe in the Lavender several times.

Prepare Your Heart and Mind

Allow your senses to take in the aroma. As you are doing this, try to put distractions out of your mind. Focus your mind on Christ. Let your mind connect the sweet smell of Lavender with the time you are spending with The Lord. Focus on His provision. Breathe slowly and deeply. Then go into a short time of prayer. Pray for whatever is on your heart. Read the verses below and pray through them. Meditate on them. Don't rush into the devotional. This part is more important. Just take a few moments to sit with The Lord.

God's Word

"Behold, I have given you every plant yielding seed that is on the face of the whole earth, and every tree with seed in its fruit. You shall have them for food." Genesis 1:29

"The Lord God took the man and put him in the Garden of Eden to work it and keep it. The Lord God commanded the man, saying, "You may surely eat of every tree of the Garden, but of the tree of the knowledge of good and evil you shall not eat, for the day that you eat of it you shall surely die." Genesis 2:15-17

"And on the banks, on both sides of the river, there will grow all kinds of trees for food. Their leaves will not wither, nor their fruit fail, but they will bear fresh fruit every month, because the water for them flows from the sanctuary. Their fruit will be for food, and their leaves for healing." Ezekiel 47:12

"Then the angel showed me the river of the water of life, bright as crystal, flowing from the throne of God and of the Lamb through the middle of the street of the city; also, on either side of the river, the tree of life with its twelve kinds of fruit, yielding its fruit each month.

The leaves of the tree were for the healing of the nations."
Revelation 22:1-2

Worth Thinking About

I'm a city boy at the very foundation of my being. I love the city. I love the constant motion, always being near people, the architecture, the sound of rushing traffic, honking horns, and zooming airplanes. I love the smell of morning smog in the summer time, and the odor that hangs in the air of recently poured tar on the road. Most of all, I love nothing more than awakening to the sound of my neighbor mowing his lawn. I don't know why. I can't explain it but I was born in the city, I've lived the majority of my life in the city, and I love the city! I believe God has put this love for the city in my heart, so that I can be where there are many people for me to share the life-giving message of the Gospel. This is a mission which I embrace completely and of which I am thankful! However, it's important for people like me to remember that when God created man, He didn't put man in a city. God put man in a garden. It's easy to read too much into that; but, it's also easy not to realize the legitimate implications of that truth. In order to more fully understand why God chose a Garden take a close look at a few things that God said to Adam and Eve when He placed them in the Garden. (*See the Genesis verses listed in the "God's Word" section.*)

There are many theologically foundational truths in these two passages. Two important foundations are: 1) that God placed Adam in the Garden with the full intention that Adam would care for the Garden and, 2) that Adam would be nourished by the fruit of the Garden. You see, according to the Biblical account of creation, man originally did not eat meat. When God placed Adam and Eve in the Garden, there were no processed foods or fast food restaurants. The nutritional needs of Adam and Eve were completely met by the fruit on the trees in that Garden. I'm not advocating against meat. Later on God did allow, and even command, the consumption of meat. My point is to say that in the earliest days of creation, before it was marred by sin and death, God fully and totally provided for the needs of man through the plants that he placed in the Garden.

Interestingly, Ezekiel 47:12 refers both BACK to Genesis 1 & 2 and FORWARD to Revelation 22. That's right, this amazing passage in Ezekiel paints a picture of both the beginning and the end. Take some time to read the entire creation account, next read the closing chapter of Revelation, then go back and read Ezekiel 17. What we read in Ezekiel 17 is what happens when the goodness of God freely flows from His throne throughout His creation. It starts as a trickling stream; but, by the time the picture is finished, it grows to a booming river of fresh water, so ravenous and potent that it even turns the Dead Sea into a fountain of life giving fresh water! It comes as no surprise that just as in the Garden of Eden, we find trees nourished by this water continuing to produce fruit month after month. These trees provide not only fruit, but in their leaves is life-giving balm of healing for the wellness of man. In this beautiful picture we see that as God is pouring out His goodness on creation, it is His intention to provide for all the needs of mankind through His creation.

As you breathe in the fragrance of Lavender and you enjoy the refreshing aroma, consider Genesis 1 & 2, Ezekiel 17, and Revelation 22. Lavender is distilled from the flower of the plant. It is known as the Swiss Army knife of essential oils; because, its uses are virtually endless. It is a food that God created to provide wellness and support to your body. As you walk around with the aroma on your body today, let it be a reminder to you of things that are to come. That God's goodness is poured out on creation and every need is met out of that goodness!

Reflections…

Spikenard

Prepare Your Surroundings

Set up a diffuser with some Spikenard in it before you start your devotion time. Let it run for a few minutes so that the aroma fills the room. Then sit down on the floor and put two drops of Spikenard on your hands and rub them together. Cup them over your nose and begin to take deep breaths, then regular breaths in and out. Let the aroma fill your senses. Now, read the Bible passage below several times and get it into your mind:

God's Word

"And while he was at Bethany in the house of Simon the leper, as he was reclining at table, a woman came with an alabaster flask of ointment of pure nard, very costly, and she broke the flask and poured it over his head. There were some who said to themselves indignantly, 'Why was the ointment wasted like that? For this ointment could have been sold for more than three hundred denarii and given to the poor.' And they scolded her. But Jesus said, 'Leave her alone. Why do you trouble her? She has done a beautiful thing to me. For you always have the poor with you, and whenever you want, you can do good for them. But you will not always have me. She has done what she could; she has anointed my body beforehand for burial.'" Mark 14:3-8

Prepare Your Heart and Mind

As your mind is taking in the content of the passage, allow the aroma to fill your sense of smell. Imagine you are in the room with Jesus looking on the scene that is playing out; then, consider this question "What am I willing to bring to Jesus?" Let your mind rest on that question for a little while and then move into reading the devotional.

Worth Thinking About

Spikenard is a soothing oil that was commonly used in New Testament times as sign of hospitality shared with guests. Traveling in the hot, dry, and sandy conditions of the Middle East would leave one's skin dry and cracked. Also, walking for miles with nothing more than sandals would leave the feet cut, blistered, and uncomfortable. Often times the only comfort a host would have to offer was a bowl of cold water to sprinkle over their guest's head and wash their feet. Those who possessed a certain standard of wealth would be able to offer water and olive oil, or olive oil and Spikenard.

Mary was probably not wealthy. Many Bible scholars believe that the bottle of Spikenard Mary used in this story was actually her dowry. In Biblical times a dowry was given to the bride by her father as a means of providing financial support in case her husband abandoned her or died before her. We don't know the marital history of Mary, but what we do know is that if this bottle of Spikenard was her dowry, then it was her only future means of providing for herself. A denarii was about a day's wage for a common worker, so this oil was worth almost an entire year's wage. In today's terms, it would probably translate to between thirty and forty thousand American dollars. This was an expensive bottle of oil!

Consider what this action tells us about Mary. She quite literally brought her most valuable possession to Jesus and poured it out for Him. There was not anything that Mary physically owned that she was not willing to give to Jesus. In this one action, she demonstrates that all of her physical possessions and wealth, whatever that would have been, were to be used for the purpose of serving Jesus. Her physical life was in His hands.

Not only did she pour out her most valuable possession for Him, but consider also, this bottle of oil was her future security. By bringing it, breaking it open, and pouring it on Jesus, she was opening herself to a potentially dangerous situation. This bottle of oil was her back up plan. As a woman in first century Jewish culture, it's not as though she could just go get a job. Generally speaking, women did not work outside the home. She was putting herself in a position where her future security was very much in jeopardy. In this action Mary put her future in Jesus' hands.

Additionally, by bringing this very expensive bottle of oil and pouring all of it on Jesus' head and feet, Mary risked making herself a social outcast. We see this in the response of the people around her. They began to lecture her about the unwise use of this expensive bottle of oil, as IF there were some possible way that anything could be wasted in the worship of Jesus. Mary was probably aware, as we are aware from reading the Gospels, that the apostles were constantly arguing among themselves about which of them was the greatest. Mary must have realized that there would be social implications for taking such an extreme action in this particular group of people, and yet Mary did it anyway. She put herself in Jesus' hands socially.

When I consider all that is wrapped up in this one act of worship, the single word that comes to my mind is, "worthy." You will note that while everyone else is rebuking her, Jesus is rebuking everyone else. He does not denounce her act of worship, rather He receives it. Even though this was a such a huge sacrifice on Mary's part, the thing that jumps out of the text loud and clear is that Jesus is worthy of this kind of worship. Mary's act of worship compels us to a self-examination of our own worship. It's not that by bringing expensive things to Jesus we give ourselves greater standing before Jesus; nothing could be further from the truth! If you have put your trust in Christ as your Savior, then you know that your salvation is completely and totally because of His goodness and mercy; it is not at all because of any good work we have done! No, we must bring the best that we have to offer to Jesus because He has made us righteous before God. He is worthy of our best. Like Mary, we must give the best we have to offer because we love Him and we trust Him, and for those reasons alone.

What does *your* worship of Jesus look like? What crazy things have *you* done for the sake of the worship of His name? Do *you* serve in small, simple, daily ways for the worship of His name? Take some time to examine your life and your worship; and then, spend next few moments in quiet worship celebrating Jesus and His goodness in your life.

Reflections…

Myrrh: The Story of Jesus' Life

Prepare Your Surroundings

Find a quiet place where you can focus your attention fully on your time with Christ. Set up your diffuser with Myrrh and let it run for a few minutes before you get started.

Prepare Your Heart and Mind

Spend time just inhaling the aroma of Myrrh. Allow your senses to experience the scent by fully relaxing. Take several long, deep breaths. Spend several moments in quiet thought considering the life of Christ. Think through what the Bible tells us of His life starting with His birth and ending at His death. Think about the parables and lessons that He taught, how He spent His time, and the untold number of people that He helped. What an amazing Life to ponder! Next, read the following passages slowly and deliberately. Start by comprehending each word, then each sentence, until you have read and understood the entire passage. Read it several times and let the concepts sink into your thoughts. Do not rush through this part. Fully consider what each passage says and how they are connected with one another.

God's Word

"And going into the house they saw the child with Mary his mother, and they fell down and worshiped Him. Then, opening their treasures, they offered Him gifts, gold and frankincense and myrrh." Mathew 2:11

"And they offered Him wine mixed with myrrh, but he did not take it." Mathew 15:23

"Nicodemus also, who earlier had come to Jesus by night, came bringing a mixture of myrrh and aloes, about seventy-five pounds in weight. So they took the body of Jesus and bound it in linen cloths with the spices, as is the burial custom of the Jews." John 19:39-40

Worth Thinking About

Of all the oils that are mentioned in the Bible, Myrrh is mentioned the most. Of all the oils that are mentioned throughout the life and ministry of Christ specifically, Myrrh again, is mentioned the most.

Not only is Myrrh mentioned more than any other oil in the life of Christ, but each time that it is mentioned, it is mentioned in the context of incredibly important moments. We can gather from this observation that the aroma of Myrrh was probably commonly present throughout the ministry of Christ. Let's take some time to look at places where Myrrh is mentioned in the life of Christ.

His Birth

Very early in the life of Jesus wise men from the East followed a prophecy and came to find Jesus. Upon finding Him they bowed down in worship and gave him gifts of gold, frankincense, and myrrh. We really don't know for sure why they chose these three items; except that, in Ancient Near Eastern culture these items were all of great value.

Think this moment through... Jesus, the Son of God, stepped out of eternity and took flesh upon Himself. Consider, even now as you sit, study, and pray, that you are breathing in the same aroma that was present in the room when the wise men came to worship Jesus.

His Death

The death of Jesus Christ is without a doubt the most important event in human history. It is the focal point of the entire narrative of Scripture. Not because the crucifixion was unique to Jesus. It wasn't. Romans crucified citizens regularly. Not because Jesus took any more physical punishment than any other person who was crucified. Roman soldiers were trained killers, and they took delight in the suffering of their victims. No, the death of Jesus is unique because while He was hanging on the cross He faced far greater pain than any Roman soldier could inflict. In this event Jesus, the perfect, sinless, Son of God, took upon Himself all of God's righteous judgment for our sin. Because He was without sin, and not deserving of death, He alone was able to die in our place. He did so willingly. He swallowed the full cup of God's wrath. And then He died.

Interestingly, in this moment, the most important moment in all of human history, the aroma of Myrrh was present. The aroma that you are breathing in as you sit in the silence of your prayer space, is one of the aroma's that was hanging in the air as the sinless Son of God died on the cross to deliver us from our sin.

As you breathe in that aroma consider what Christ did for you and me in that moment. The Bible teaches that we are all breakers of God's law. Where God says, "Thou shall not bear false witness," we've told lies. Where God says, "Thou shall not take my name in vain," we have used His name as a curse word. Where God says, "Thou shall not steal," we have taken what doesn't belong to us. And worst of all, where God says, "Thou shall have no other god before me," we have worshiped other gods besides Him. Probably not in the form of little statues, but in the form of things we worship in our culture. Money. Sex. Power. Influence. We have worshiped these things over God. And, we stand condemned before Him. God is a Holy God that must punish our sin. If God judges us according to the standard of His righteous law we will all be found guilty. But in that moment, as Jesus was hanging on the cross, He displayed the fullness of God's love, grace, and mercy when He willingly took the punishment for our sins. Let the aroma connect you to that moment and take some time to weigh what Christ did for you.

If you've never trusted Christ, know this, you don't need to face the judgment of God. Jesus died in your place. The Bible says that if you turn from your sin and trust in what Christ did on the cross, God will forgive you and will invite you into His Kingdom. Go to God now. There aren't any magical words. Confess your sin to Him, turn from your sin, and put your trust in Christ. The Bible says that if you do this God will make you a new creation, you will be reborn, and He will change your life. For support, contact your closest friend that is a Christian and share with them what you have done. They will be able to help you learn how to be a follower of Christ!

His Burial and Resurrection

But the story doesn't end with the death of Jesus. A man named Joseph took Christ's body and gave it to Nicodemus to be prepared for burial. Nicodemus used 75 pounds worth of Myrrh and Aloes (Sandalwood) to prepare Jesus' body for burial. That's a lot of oil with a lot of aroma! Then Nicodemus covered the body of Jesus with burial clothes and left the tomb.

On Sunday Mary (Magdalene) went to the tomb to finish preparing Jesus' body for burial. She discovered that the tomb was open, and His body was missing! As Mary approached the tomb of Jesus, where Nicodemus had just used 75 pounds of Myrrh and Aloes, the aroma of Myrrh would have been very thick in the air. Consider that you are breathing in the *same aroma* that Mary, Peter, and John smelled when they entered the empty tomb of Jesus. Take some time to consider the surreal nature of that truth.

Ponder what was accomplished by the resurrection of Jesus as you breathe in the aroma of Myrrh. In His death, Jesus paid the penalty for sin. In His resurrection, Jesus completely and totally defeated death and sin. Now, for those who have trusted in Him, our wickedness was transferred to Him in His death. In His resurrection His goodness is transferred to us. So, when God the Father looks down from His throne upon us He sees the goodness of His Son. In His resurrection from the dead, Jesus displayed the full glory of God's grace and we are the beneficiaries of that!

From now on whenever you smell the aroma of Myrrh let the aroma take your mind to the sacrifice of Christ. That, though He was God, He became a man so that He might live a sinless life; and then, He died on the cross to deliver us from our sin to the glory of God the Father. Take some time now, before you finish, to think about Jesus. Let the aroma of Myrrh guide your mind to Him. Think about His birth, His death, and His resurrection. Think about the fact that His sacrifice is your only way of salvation. Finally, spend some time thanking Him and celebrating the goodness of God in the Gospel of Christ.

Reflections…

Cassia - The Oil of Unity

Prepare Your Surroundings

Find a quiet place. Open a bottle of Cassia and hold it up to your nose. Slowly inhale and exhale the aroma. Allow it to fill your senses. Put a few drops on your hands and rub them together, then cup them over your nose. Take several long deep breaths. Give yourself several minutes to take in the aroma.

Prepare Your Heart and Mind

Now, read the following passage. Take time to understand what the passage is saying. Let your mind dwell on it to get the concepts in your head.

Next, spend some time praying for your brothers and sisters in Christ. Start with those who attend your local church. Pray for each fellow member you can think of by name. Consider what is going on in their life and pray for any needs they may have that you are aware of. Pray for other Christians you know who do not attend your church. Pray for brothers and sisters in other parts of the world. Pray for the missionaries that are taking the Gospel to difficult places. Pray for the people who live in those difficult places. Pray for fellow Christians who are being persecuted for their faith. This is important; so, don't rush through it.

God's Word

"Behold, how good and pleasant it is when brothers dwell in unity! It is like the precious oil on the head, running down on the beard, on the beard of Aaron, running down on the collar of his robes! It is like the dew of Hermon, which falls on the mountains of Zion! For there the Lord has commanded the blessing, life forevermore." Psalm 133:1-3

Worth Thinking About

Do you have people that you just like being together with? I grew up in a family that got together a lot. We got together for Christmas, Easter, Mother's Day, Father's Day, Labor Day, Memorial Day, Independence Day, birthdays, weddings, and all kinds of other happy stuff. These occasions were always big deals in my family. We also got together when difficult things happened. When someone was in the hospital we were all there praying for them and ready to help. When someone passed away, everyone came to the funeral. No excuses. We were all there. I come from a very close extended family. In my childhood we were always together. Not because we had to be, it was because we wanted to be together. We were together on purpose. We enjoyed being around each other. I have good relationships even to this day with second and third cousins. We have done a lot of life together and I enjoy them. Spending so much time together has created strong bonds that still exist today.

The Bible has a lot to say about God's people being together. God created us to be in relationships with one another. The Christian faith works itself out in the context of Christian community. With that thought in mind, the above passage presents an interesting element about togetherness of the people of God. The author tells us that the gathering of the people of God is both pleasant and precious; and, he uses the Holy Anointing Oil of Exodus 30 to illustrate his point. Just as the oil that was poured on Aaron when he was anointed is pleasant and precious, so also is the gathering of the people of God.

The oil is pleasant. Here the author is talking about the aroma of the oil. The blend of oils used in Holy Anointing Oil has a very sweet and pleasing smell. The author is connecting this pleasant aroma with the gathering of the people of God. Just as the oil gives off a pleasant aroma, so the gathering of the people of God is a pleasant gathering. Ponder that idea for a moment. Would you consider your time of gathering with other believers to be a pleasant time? Do you personally make a pleasant contribution to the gathering? Are the words nice when you gather? Is your demeanor agreeable as you go about serving our Lord? It should be noted that this pleasant environment doesn't spring up out of thin air. On the contrary, the pleasant nature of a Christian gathering is a direct outgrowth of the Spirit of God working joy in the hearts of His people. Where there is no joy, pleasantry is simply that, only a pleasantry. Just as the aroma you are breathing in is a pleasant aroma, God intends for the gathering of His people to be a pleasant gathering.

Not only is the oil pleasant, but it is also precious. It is precious because it is very costly to make. Each of the oils that went into the making of the Holy Anointing Oil would have come at a great price and would have been difficult to come by. There was no auto ship program in the time of Moses. Those oils could only be purchased when certain traders traveled through town on a specific trade route. It was no convenient task to gain access to such fine oils. They were rare and expensive; therefore, they were precious.

The same thing is true of God's people. They are very precious to God because they were purchased at a high price. A price much higher than the price of an expensive oil or any other created luxury! The people of God were purchased at the high price of the blood of His Son. This is the message of the Gospel: that we were once slaves to sin; however, God, because He is rich in mercy, forgave our sins and purchased us back because Christ died in our place. Our penalty has been paid by a price that is beyond our comprehension! If you have never come to know Christ as your Savior, then see the devotion on Myrrh for more information.

Since Jesus died to bring us into His family, then we need to view each other as precious possessions of our King! Spend some time today considering how you view the people of God. Think on it. Pray on it. Ask God to show you where your heart truly is.

Reflections…

Grounding

Prepare Your Surroundings

Find a quiet place and set up your diffuser with Grounding essential oil blend from Young Living. Let the diffuser run for a few minutes before you get started. Now breathe in the aroma before you begin praying.

Prepare Your Heart and Mind

Spend some time thinking about the people who God has placed in your life that speak wisdom to you and help you grow in your walk with The Lord. It may help to write a list. Think of all the ways they have helped you over the time you've known them. Pray for them and thank God for allowing them to be a part of your life. As you are thinking about those people, spend some time reading over the following verse. Take your time and read it repeatedly to give you a clear understanding of its meaning. I encourage you not to rush this part. Consider this verse in light of all of the people whom God has provided to speak wisdom into your life and how you receive their counsel.

God's Word

"Let a righteous man strike me—it is a kindness; let him rebuke me— it is oil for my head; let my head not refuse it. Yet my prayer is continually against their evil deeds." Psalm 141:5

Worth Thinking About

No one likes to be told they're wrong, especially in our culture. Being told we are wrong, or there may be a better way than our way, offends our sense of western individualism. One of the things we see repeated throughout the Bible is that those who are wise are the ones who listen to and seek wise counsel. This reality was illuminated for me at a time when my wife and I were in a bind and the only options on the table were varying degrees of bad. We had just moved into a new apartment and we had a terrible leak in the ceiling (which was more like a flood). The apartment complex had fixed the leak twice and it was leaking again, for the third time in a week. Every time this happened, our carpet would become soaked and the apartment community would have to bring in big fans to dry the floor. Because of this "leak," my wife and I were having to stay with my parents. One day I ran back to the house to pick something up and I noticed it was really cold. I went over to the thermostat, which was set to 69, but the temperature was only 53 in the apartment. I messed with it for a little while and eventually discovered that it wasn't working. I called the apartment complex only to discover that they knew the problem existed and were not going to be able to fix it for another 2 weeks! They had "ordered a part"...right... and what was I supposed to do to provide shelter to my wife and two young children for the next two weeks? The apartment manager informed me, in no uncertain terms, that this situation was not her problem. That night I was talking through the options with my dad. We were less than a month into the lease. We didn't have the money to move again, I couldn't afford to pay the fee to break the lease, and yet, I couldn't see continuing to live in a place where we couldn't "live." My dad kept trying to explain to me that there may be other options on the table; but, I couldn't see how those options were possible. Finally, after hours of circular conversations, my dad looked at me and said "Son, there are only two ways that you learn things in this world. You can learn from the mistakes and life experience of others, or you go through every stupid decision yourself. Life is going to be very painful for you and your family if you continue to choose to do things the second way." The next day I agreed to call an attorney, who was ultimately able to help resolve the situation swiftly. I've always remembered that conversation with my dad. Whether he realized it or not, my dad was giving me advice that comes straight from the Bible.

Because I chose to receive the rebuke and wise counsel of my father, I was able to handle the situation and take care of my family. I believe that is what David is saying in our text. This link between oil on the head and the rebuke of a righteous man is a very interesting connection. Often times in Ancient Near Eastern culture, a host would anoint the head of visitors providing comfort to them after having traveled in hot, dry conditions all day. When David says here that the rebuke of a righteous man is like oil upon his head, he is saying that when someone speaks wisdom into his life it is comforting and refreshing to him. I don't know about you, but comfort is not a word that I generally think of first in relationship to rebuke; however, for those who are striving to walk in righteousness, the correction of a friend can be very comforting. Consider the following verses:

Proverbs 8:33

"Hear instruction and be wise, and do not neglect it."

Proverbs 10:8

"The wise of heart will receive commandments, but a babbling fool will come to ruin."

Proverbs 13:20

"Whoever walks with the wise becomes wise, but the companion of fools will suffer harm."

Proverbs 21:11

"When a scoffer is punished, the simple becomes wise; when a wise man is instructed, he gains knowledge."

You will notice all of those verses come from the book of Proverbs. That means they are all written by Solomon. Scripture teaches that he was the wisest man ever to live. To be clear, these are just four examples. You can find this concept of 'wisdom that comes from listening' throughout Proverbs. The repeated admonition of Scripture is to seek out and listen to wise counsel.

Today you are diffusing Grounding in conjunction with your devotion. Grounding is an oil blend that is designed to promote stability and wise decision making in the midst of chaos. As you breathe in its aroma, take time to consider that God has provided another tool to help promote wise decision making in this life; and, that tool is the wise counsel of Godly, righteous people whom He has placed in our lives. Often times we make unnecessary, foolish decisions and learn things the hard way. Going forward we need to seek out wise counsel and save ourselves some pain! Who are the godly counselors that the Lord has placed in your path? Look for them, ask them questions, invite their input, celebrate their experience, and then see how God uses them to transform your life!

Reflections…

Peace and Calming®

Prepare Your Surroundings

Find a nice quiet place. Set up your diffuser with the Young Living blend of Peace and Calming®. Allow the diffusor to run in the room for a few moments before you get started.

Prepare Your Heart and Mind

Take time to focus your heart and mind on Christ. One of the titles that is given to Jesus in the Bible is "Prince of Peace." Think about Jesus from this perspective. Spend some time in adoration and gratefulness to Christ for all of the ways that He has brought peace into your life. Name some of them specifically. Next, read the following passage. Don't rush. Read it a few times, slowly. First considering the meaning of each word individually. Then consider what they mean as they combine into thoughts and sentences. Make sure you have a good understanding of the passage before you move on.

God's Word

"Let your reasonableness be known to everyone. The Lord is at hand; do not be anxious about anything, but in everything by prayer and supplication with thanksgiving let your requests be made known to God. And the peace of God, which surpasses all understanding, will guard your hearts and your minds in Christ Jesus." Philippians 4:5-7

Worth Thinking About

I can't even count the number of people who have sat across from me in various situations with weary eyes, slumped shoulders, and lifeless expressions. They were exhausted and empty-handed from their pursuit of peace. Peace, like happiness and many other descriptors that we use to label a successful life, is very elusive and largely undefined.

One of the reasons that peace is so elusive is that it is impossible to find peace when it is what you are pursuing. In other words, if your life goal is pursuing peace as an ultimate end, you will never be satisfied. Peace is not an ultimate thing or an ultimate good; and, it is not in itself a sufficient purpose for living one's life. On the contrary, peace comes as a result of pursuing, resting in, and trusting in *Christ*.

It's interesting to note that our Bible passage was written by the Apostle Paul to the church in Philippi while he was sitting in a jail cell for proclaiming the Gospel. This was not a man who lived a "peaceful" life by any external standards. Yet, he was a man of great peace. How could this be? He explains how in today's verse. He is not a man seeking peace, rather he is a man resting and trusting in God. Paul had been through so much in his pursuit of Christ. By this point, he had the kind of peace that comes from not just trusting God to bring a certain result, but rather he trusted God to decide what the result should be; and, Paul was satisfied with the result regardless of what it was. That is real peace!

So how do you get that kind of peace? You give your life fully to God and completely rest in His hands. That's hard. I can promise you that being a sold-out follower of Christ will not result in the easy going, nothing ever goes wrong, you never have to leave your comfort zone kind of life. Christ brings all of His followers to difficult crossroads and challenges that, if not for His grace, would be impossible. And yet, there is an indescribable peace in knowing that your life is in the pierced hands of the One who went to the cross and died for your sin. In that there is peace.

As you breathe in the amazing aroma of peace that ministers to the temporal, physical needs of your body and brings comfort in times of anxiety, allow your heart and mind to connect that aroma with the peace of God in the midst of your daily life. Let this aroma be a physical reality that compels you to consider a deeper reality of the peace that comes from resting in and trusting in Christ. Instead of a peace that is of this world, reflect upon a peace that transcends the things of this world, a peace that is beyond all human understanding.

Reflections…

The Aroma of Christ

Prepare Your Surroundings

Find a quiet place to spend in prayer. Open a bottle of Valor® (or Valor 2, both are blends produced by Young Living). Hold the bottle under your nose and take several breaths. Put a drop on your hands and rub them together. Now cup them over your nose and take several deep breaths. Next, rub the Valor® on the back and front of your neck so that the aroma fills your sense of smell during your entire worship time. Set the bottle of Valor® close by, with the lid off, while you are doing your devotional. Make sure to put the lid back on when you are finished!

Prepare Your Heart and Mind

Now read the following Bible passage. Take your time and read it slowly. Read it several times. Consider each word, then each phrase, and then each sentence. Ponder the meaning. What message is the author trying to convey? Meditate on it. Try to push every thought out of your mind and focus on this passage of Scripture. Let it fill your mind. Pray through it, and ask The Lord to help you understand its meaning. Make this your priority before you move on. Do not rush to the next part. Let God's word move from your mind to your heart. Understand the message, and then embrace it to be true.

God's Word

"But thanks be to God, who in Christ always leads us in the triumphal procession and through us spread the fragrance of the knowledge of Him everywhere. For we are the aroma of Christ to God among those who are being saved and among those who are perishing, to one a fragrance from death to death, to the other a fragrance from life to life." 2 Corinthians 2:14-16

Worth Thinking About

Is there anything more fun than victory? I learned this in real life when I was in middle school. I was on the football team and we played against our cross-town rival in the high school stadium. It was a hard-fought game. In fact, there were significant injuries for both teams through the course of the game. The game was very tight at 6 to 7 going into the fourth quarter. We were down by one point! I remember watching the coach pace the side lines, jumping in celebration with my teammates every time something good happened, and groaning like the wind was knocked out of us every time something bad happened. In the last three minutes of the game we were still down by one. Two of our best players had been injured and several of our offensive players were playing on defense. Our opponents had the ball and were close to scoring. Their quarterback stepped back to pass when our quarterback, who was now playing defense, read the play and intercepted the ball! Our side line erupted with excitement. Our coach gave one of the most motivating pep talks I had ever heard in a quick 30 seconds before our offense was back on the field. The first two plays were runs that went nowhere. The third play was an incomplete pass. It was fourth down with less than 2 minutes left. If we punted the ball, we might not get it back. If we went for it and didn't get the first down, the game would be over. The coach decided to go for it and called a passing play. Our quarterback dropped back for what seemed like an eternity, then threw the ball. The receiver caught the ball, missed one tackle and then ran the ball all the way to the end zone! I don't know that I have ever seen celebration like the one on our side line that day! It was the kind of moment that makes you wish for a way to bottle that excitement and save it for another day. It was a very fun moment.

I think that is the kind of celebration Paul is referring to in our passage. He is painting a picture of an ancient tradition. When a battle had been won, the general and his army would march through town celebrating, burning incense, and inviting the community to celebrate with them. This incense aroma was the smell of victory to the town's people! Paul is alluding to the fact that when Christ rose from the dead He won a great victory! Jesus took upon Himself all of the penalty for sin through His perfect sacrifice. In His death He paid that penalty and in His resurrection He overcame death itself. What a great victory! This victory is the basis of our faith. Paul's point in bringing up this image is to say that as we go about our lives, being transformed by Gospel through the work of the Holy Spirit, we are like a parade celebrating Christ's victory over sin and death every place that we go. **We are the aroma of His victory!**

Today you are enjoying the essential oil blend of Valor. As you breathe in that aroma take some time to consider the victory that we have in Christ. Sometimes it doesn't feel like a victory yet; because the battle is still happening in us, between our flesh and His Spirit, and around us as the world fights against God. That's because we are in a time period that theologians call the "already, but not yet." Christ's victory was completely won through His death on the cross and His resurrection. However, the victory hasn't yet been fully realized until He returns again.

Breathe in the Valor® and let its aroma be a reminder to you that God is working in you, through Christ, to make you a trophy of His grace. Let the thought of His victory give you strength to celebrate His goodness even in the most difficult of circumstances.

Reflections…

Essential Oils and the Glory of God

Prepare Your Surroundings

Select your favorite essential oil, or an oil you are in the mood for today. Set your diffuser up with that oil; then leave it running for a few minutes before you start your devotion time. Spend some time just enjoying the aroma. Consider why you enjoy that aroma. What is it about this aroma that sets it apart from others? Focus your full attention on the aroma and take in several deep breaths.

Prepare Your Heart and Mind

Move into a time of quiet prayer. Thank God for your journey over the last 14 days and spend some time celebrating the things you have considered and learned as you pray. Focus on the concept that you, including your senses, were created for the purpose of worshiping and glorifying God; and, He has redeemed you as a trophy of His grace! Consider God's goodness in giving you a sense of smell as you take in the aroma that now surrounds you. Spend some time reading over the following passage several times. Think about each word's meaning, then consider each thought, then each sentence until you get the whole meaning of the text. Don't rush this part. Prayer and Scripture reading have been the most important elements of these devotions. Once you are ready, then move on.

God's Word

"He is the image of the invisible God, the firstborn of all creation. For by Him all things were created, in heaven and on earth, visible and invisible, whether thrones or dominions or rulers or authorities - all things were created through Him and for Him." Colossians 1:15-16

Worth Thinking About

We began our journey together with a discussion of worship, and it seems fitting that we end our time together with a discussion of worship. Our Scripture reading for today was quoted in that first devotion. I'm bringing it up again because it is foundational to understand that God created all things for the purpose of His own glory! All that there ever was, is, or is to be is through Christ and for Christ!

Consider the following analogy for a moment: Say you walk into your kitchen while someone is baking a fresh batch of your favorite cookies. As you walk into the kitchen you notice that your mind immediately has a positive response to the aroma. A number of things may happen. Your mind may go back to a memory that it associates with that aroma. Your mouth may begin to salivate in anticipation of enjoying some freshly baked cookies. Depending upon how positively your mind responds to the aroma you may even get a tingly feeling in the pit of your stomach! Here is what I want you to understand about that moment, both the aroma and your body's response to the aroma are for the glory of God.

But how exactly does the aroma, and your body's response to the aroma, bring glory to God in that moment? I'm glad you asked me that question! You see, we don't "bring glory to God" by adding any glory to Him. In fact, His glory is the very standard from which the definition of glory flows. When we talk about bringing glory to God we are talking about drawing attention to His goodness. When we enjoy a taste, an aroma, or a texture each of these moments is a reminder of His goodness. God is glorified when the things that bring about joy in our life remind us of His goodness.

This idea of using our senses to enhance our worship of God is almost entirely lost on the Western evangelical church. I am hoping that these devotions raised your awareness of how your senses may enhance your worship time daily. Essential oils are just a tool that we've used over these last 14 days to engage you in thinking about worship in conjunction with your sense of smell. The main thing I hope you take away from this book is that God has blessed you with senses so that you may enjoy them in Him; and, through this joy bring glory to His name!

As you finish your journey take some time to celebrate your enriched understanding of how God's gift of senses can be an important part of worship. Spend a few more minutes enjoying the essential oil aroma that you are diffusing. Allow the goodness and the joy of this aroma to remind you of the goodness of God. Take this time to celebrate God's goodness in creating you in such a way that even your senses point you back to His goodness.

Reflections…

Appendix A

This section is to help those who don't own the specific oils called for in a devotional. We have tried to make a combination of blends and singles available as recommendations for each devotion. We tried to pick specific oils that are very common, that we would anticipate most people to have. In places where singles are included to replace blends, our intent is to include readers that are not necessarily Young Living oil users. Though we recommend that you use Young Living, because Young Living provides the highest standards for essential oil purity through the Seed to Seal guarantee; none the less, we still want to include you even if you do not choose to use Young Living.

1. Holy Anointing Oil: Exodus II, Thieves®, Frankincense
2. The Gift Giver: Any Citrus Oil
3. Frankincense: Tea Tree
4. Sacred Mountain: Frankincense, Stress Away
5. Oil of Gladness: Joy™, Stress Away, Lemon
6. Hyssop: Purification®, Peppermint
7. Lavender: Lemon
8. Spikenard: Frankincense
9. Myrrh: Tee Tree, Frankincense
10. Cassia: Peppermint
11. Grounding: Stress Away, Peace and Calming®, Tea Tree
12. Peace and Calming: Stress Away, Lavender
13. Aroma of Christ: Joy™, Frankincense, Lemon
14. Essential Oils & The Glory of God – Oil of your choice

CPSIA information can be obtained
at www.ICGtesting.com
Printed in the USA
BVHW041834031218
534673BV00018B/329/P